CONQUERING
ANXIETY & DEPRESSION

YOUR ROADMAP TO PERMANENT HEALING
WITHOUT MEDS*

Table of Contents

- Anxiety & depression nearly killed me

- It haunted and dis-able me from childhood

- I always thought I was to blame; never felt comfortable and at ease

- It left me angry, resentful, full of shame, and full of fear

- I finally had enough; I was determined to "fix" it

- It was worth the struggle; I grew stronger & empowered by it

- Today, I'm spreading the message of hope & possibility for you!

21-DAY HAPPINESS
WORKOUT & KICKSTART
M. Fenton Deutsch
REVOLUTIONARY, NEW WAY
TO BEAT THE BLUES
& TRANSFORM YOUR LIFE

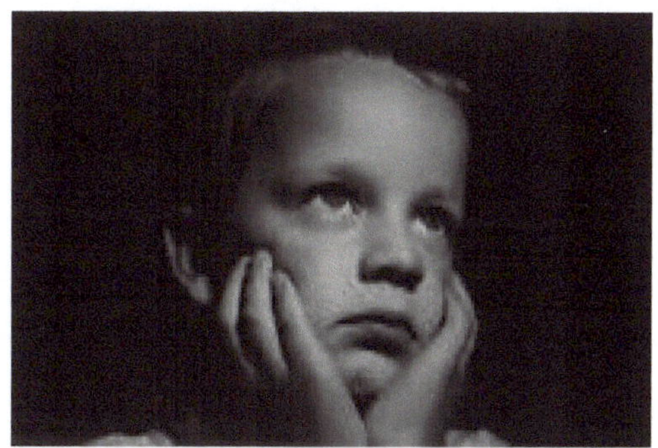

Mitch Before @ Age 55

Mitch After @ Age 62

• 310 lbs.	• 199 lbs.
• *On 15 Medications	• *Medication Free
• Walking with a cane	• *Workout 5 days/week – totally buff
• Workaholic	• Doing what I love with total balance
• Addicted to Alcohol & Pills	• Substance Free
• Kids & ex-wife hate me	• Healed relationships with Family & Friends
• Few Friends	• Deep & Loving Friendships at home and at work.
• Angry & Burnt Out	• Free from my past and living in the incredible flow and gifts of my life.
• Lonely, Irritable, Discontent	• Meditate & do Yoga, Spin & Cross Fit
• Couch Potato	• Happy, fulfilled & smiling, relaxed & truly grateful to be alive! At peace with my life & the universe
• Very Sad & Mad	

- Anxiety & Depression are able & powerful foes

- They are not your enemy, but signposts that something has to change

- You must learn to process your life entirely differently – better!

- You can learn the tools & skills that have already helped so many of us

- You can change those parts of you that no longer serve you

- You can live your life free from the bondage of anxiety, depression, & fear

- You are good enough, worth it, and...yes you, too can achieve well-being/peace-of-mind

- We can do this together, if you want it enough

- Suspend your belief that you will fail; Believe that I believe you can do this

- Stop judging your yourself/your past, fearing the future;

- Become really honest, open-minded, and willing to do what it takes

- Take massive action and focus on winning a day-at-a-time

- Stop judging your past failures and frustrations, just stay focused on the prize freedom

- Surrender to the process, accept progress & master your "perfect imperfections"

DISCLAIMERS & CAUTIONS

- Disclaimer: there is so much pain to be faced with inner child work. be done treating your anxiety and depression. If you need professional help, get it now. At bottom of when treating your anxiety and depression.

- These exercises are NOT intended to replace therapy, programs or groups for the inner child or child abuse. If you've gone through child sexual abuse, severe emotional abuse, or have a mental illness, seeking professional help is essential. This course is only meant to be a supplement. Finally, I truly hope you find something in this course that will nourish you and give you the courage to deal with and manage your own anxiety and/or depression.

- if you experience strange or overwhelming emotions while practicing the advice below, please stop immediately. Seek the help of a professional counselor before proceeding.

- Remember that everything takes time. The practices we'll review later are not quick fixes. They're not sparkly wands that will immediately make everything better. But they will give you the basic tools you need for feeling safe, secure, and protected at a core level. I truly hope you find something in this course that will nourish you and your relationship with your inner child.

- How they impact us? How do you know if you have them?

- How do you identify what needs healing in you?

- Most effective transformational healing strategies

- Heroes Stories

- How to take back & reclaim you're your life

- Anxiety is a normal and often healthy emotion. However, when a person regularly feels disproportionate levels of anxiety, it might become a medical disorder. Anxiety disorders form a category of mental health diagnoses that lead to excessive nervousness, fear, apprehension, and worry.

- When you're feeling anxious or stressed, your body releases stress hormones, such as adrenaline and cortisol. These cause the physical symptoms of anxiety, such as an increased heart rate and increased sweating. Physical symptoms can include: a pounding heartbeat.

- Types of Anxiety Disorders: Generalized Anxiety Disorder. ...Obsessive-Compulsive Disorder (OCD) ...Panic Disorder. ...Post-Traumatic Stress Disorder (PTSD) ...Social Phobia (or Social Anxiety Disorder)

- Panic Attacks can be serious and can lead to major illness

- More Detailed Profile of Anxiety: Click here: https://www.mayoclinic.org/diseases-conditions/anxiety/symptoms-causes/syc-20350961 Anxiety Disorders affect 18.1 percent of adults in the United States (approximately 40 million adults between the ages of 18 to 54). - National Institute of Mental Health (NIMH).Apr 2, 2019

- ·Current estimates put this number much higher - approximately 30 percent - as many people don't seek help, are misdiagnosed, or don't know they have issues with anxiety.

- According to The Economic Burden of Anxiety Disorders, a study commissioned by the ADAA and based on data gathered by the association and published in the Journal of Clinical Psychiatry, anxiety disorders cost the U.S. more than $42 billion a year, almost one third of the $148 billion total mental health bill for the U.S.

- More than $22.84 billion of those costs are associated with the repeated use of healthcare services, as those with anxiety disorders seek relief for symptoms that mimic physical illnesses.

- People with an anxiety disorder are three-to-five times more likely to go to the doctor and six times more likely to be hospitalized for psychiatric disorders than non-sufferers

- Anxiety disorders are the most common mental illness in the U.S., affecting 40 million adults in the United States age 18 and older, or 18.1% of the population every year.

- Anxiety disorders are highly treatable, yet only 36.9% of those suffering receive treatment.

- People with an anxiety disorder are three to five times more likely to go to the doctor and six times more likely to be hospitalized for psychiatric disorders than those who do not suffer from anxiety disorders.

- Anxiety disorders develop from a complex set of risk factors, including genetics, brain chemistry, personality, and life events.

- Famous people who have been impacted by depression and anxiety:

- https://www.elle.com/culture/celebrities/news/g29945/celebrities-depression-anxiety-mental-health/

- https://www.socialworkdegreeguide.com/30-famous-people-alive-today-battled-depression/

- "Americans are 10 times more likely to have depressive illness than they were 60 years ago…and a recent study found the rate of depression has more than doubled in just the past decade".

- Globally, things aren't much better; according to the World Health Organization (WHO) 450 million people worldwide are directly affected by mental disorders and disabilities and that by 2030 depression will top the list of all other health conditions as the number one financial burden around the world.

- Suicide, addiction, loneliness, despair are at all time highs – especially with young people in fact – epidemic and epic!

Symptoms

- While a number of different diagnoses constitute anxiety disorders, the symptoms of generalized anxiety disorder (GAD) will often include the following:

- restlessness, and a feeling of being "on-edge"

- uncontrollable feelings of worry

- increased irritability

- concentration difficulties

- sleep difficulties, such as problems in falling or staying asleep

- While these symptoms might be normal to experience in daily life, people with GAD will experience them to persistent or extreme levels. GAD may present as vague, unsettling worry or a more severe anxiety that disrupts day-to-day living.

- https://www.youtube.com/watch?v=iALfvFpcItE

- https://www.youtube.com/watch?v=SDPW3pdlnLk

HOW ANXIETY AFFECTS YOUR LIFE

- Social anxiety disorder prevents you from living your life. You'll avoid situations that most people consider "normal." You might even have a hard time understanding how others can handle them so easily.

- When you avoid all or most social situations, it affects your personal relationships. It can also lead to:

- Low self-esteem

- Negative thoughts

- Depression

- Sensitivity to criticism

- Poor social skills that don't improve

- Inability to be intimate and form healthy relationships

- Can result in addictions (substance & behavioral) and incredible loneliness, hopelessness, poor self-esteem, image, worth++

- You feel out of sorts and you know it. You can't explain why, but know deep down something is not right. You feel uncomfortable in your own skin, not centered and are full of fear, sadness, and have trouble seeing the world realistically. Your coping skills – or lack thereof – don't work. You may feel out of control. You always may need help and should be evaluated by a professional.

- This short quiz will help you quantify and better read your particular situation: Self-Diagnostic: Take the Mood Disorder Quiz: https://www.nhs.uk/conditions/stress-anxiety-depression/mood-self-assessment/

- https://www.depression-anxiety-stress-test.org/take-the-test.html

Worldwide Statistics

- Depression is the leading cause of disability worldwide. Almost 75% of people with mental disorders remain untreated in developing countries with almost 1 million people taking their lives each year. In addition, according to the World Health Organization (WHO), 1 in 13 globally suffers from anxiety. The WHO reports that anxiety disorders are the most common mental disorders worldwide with specific phobia, major depressive disorder and social phobia being the most common anxiety disorders.2

WHAT IS DEPRESSION?

- While we all feel sad, moody or low from time to time, some people experience these feelings intensely, for long periods of time (weeks, months or even years) and sometimes without any apparent reason. Depression is more than just a low mood – it's a serious condition that affects your physical and mental health.

- https://www.youtube.com/watch?v=GOK1tKFFIQI

- https://www.youtube.com/watch?v=si8zkfhM5n0

- https://www.healthline.com/health/depression-best-videos-of-the-year#2

- https://www.ted.com/talks?topics%5B%5D=depression

- Caused by combination of recent events and other long-term personal factors:

- Life Events: long-term unemployment, abusive environment, prolonged work stress

- Personal Factors: Family history (depression can run in families), Personality (prone to excessive worry, self-critical, negative, overly sensitive)

- Serious Mental Illness: stress & worry of coping with serious illness or overwhelming situation.

- Drugs & Alcohol: can lead to and cause/exacerbate depression and chemical imbalance

- The signs and symptoms of depression include loss of interest in activities that were once interesting or enjoyable, including sex; loss of appetite, with weight loss, or overeating, with weight gain; loss of emotional expression (flat affect); a persistently sad, anxious, or empty mood; feelings of hopelessness, pessimism, guilt, worthlessness, or helplessness; social withdrawal; unusual fatigue, low energy level, a feeling of being slowed down; sleep disturbance and insomnia, early-morning awakening or oversleeping; trouble concentrating, remembering, or making decisions; unusual restlessness or irritability; persistent physical problems such as headaches, digestive disorders, or chronic pain that do not respond to treatment, and thoughts of death or suicide or suicide attempts. The principal types of depression are called major depression, dysthymia, and bipolar disease (manic-depressive disease).

- 1. Physical pain

- 2. Grouchy is your new normal

- 3. You drink more alcohol than normal

- 4. Big changes in weight

- 5. You forgot to shower (again)

- 6. You can't make up your mind

- 7. You feel really, really overwhelmed with guilt

- Depression occurs more often in women than men. Some differences in the manner in which the depressed mood manifests has been found based on sex and age. In men it manifests often as tiredness, irritability and anger. They may show more reckless behavior and abuse drugs and alcohol. They also tend to not recognize that they are depressed and fail to seek help. In women depression tends to manifest as sadness, worthlessness, and guilt. In younger children depression is more likely to manifest as school refusal, anxiety when separated from parents, and worry about parents dying. Depressed teenagers tend to be irritable, sulky, and get into trouble in school. They also frequently have co-morbid anxiety, eating disorders, or substance abuse. In older adults depression may manifest more subtly as they tend to be less likely to admit to feelings of sadness or grief and medical illnesses which are more common in this population also contributes or causes the depression.

CAN YOU HAVE BOTH ANXIETY & DEPRESSION?

- Anxiety & Depression are different conditions

- Have similar treatments

- Anxiety can be caused by depression and vice versa

- in both depression and anxiety, irritability, decreased concentration and impaired sleep are common.

- It is not uncommon to experience occasional and brief periods of feeling down and anxious. These episodes are not usually a cause for concern, and once passed, you are able to resume life as usual.

- Being depressed often makes us anxious, and anxiety often makes us depressed.

- If it turns out that you have both conditions, there are lots of ways to get help.

Sources:

- https://www.ted.com/playlists/287/4_ted_talks_on_overcoming_depr

- https://www.ted.com/talks/andrew_solomon_depression_the_secret_we_share?referrer=playlist-4_ted_talks_on_overcoming_depr

- https://www.ted.com/talks/nikki_webber_allen_don_t_suffer_from_your_depression_in_silence?referrer=playlist-4_ted_talks_on_overcoming_depr

- https://www.ted.com/talks/kevin_breel_confessions_of_a_depressed_comic?referrer=playlist-4_ted_talks_on_overcoming_depr

- https://www.ted.com/talks/ruby_wax_what_s_so_funny_about_mental_illness?referrer=playlist-4_ted_talks_on_overcoming_depr

anxiety ted talks

- https://www.youtube.com/watch?v=A1anXJhVamc

- https://jodiaman.com/blog/tedx-talks-anxiety-panic/

- https://www.ted.com/talks/olivia_remes_how_to_cope_with_anxiety?language=en

- https://www.ted.com/talks/olivia_remes_how_to_cope_with_anxiety?language=en

- Increased quality of life

- Have a full, meaningful, purposeful, happy, joyful life

- Allows you to grow normally, grow up normally

- Trauma of anxiety & depression can lead to major life growth if overcome/managed

- Help others deal and heal from anxiety and depression disorders

- Ward off further possible negative effects of discomfort and dis-ease, diminished health and even disease and/or premature death

- With work and treatment, you can live a full and normal life!

- There are many ways to medically treat anxiety and/or depression. As we are neither doctors or psychologists, we will not address the medical issues and treatment options in this course. The link below will provide you with a good start to understanding your options. : https://adaa.org/finding-help/treatment/medication

- https://www.samhsa.gov/find-treatment

- https://www.webmd.com/anxiety-panic/guide/medications-treat-mental-disorders#1

We will be addressing non-medical forms of treatment and the tools we use to process our lives differently. As I no longer use any mood altering substances by choice, I have take more alternative non-medication approaches such as cognitive (learning how to challenge irrational feelings) , emotional and behavioral modification, 12-Step and other addiction treatment programs, and a complete spiritual reboot to help heal and stay that way. While it may not be for your (and you should always consult a medical or mental professional), these are the very same tools that many of us have used to heal and manage/eliminate both anxiety and depression from our lives. That is the purpose for The Healing Academy and this course.

- First a word of caution. Both anxiety and depression are complex issues and no two cases are necessarily alike. You may have a mild case of either, both or be totally debilitated as a result of your symptoms. Any treatment you choose may be multi-faceted (meds, therapy, behavioral changes), as it was mine in the beginning. I took copious amounts and different types of anti-depressant and anti-anxiety medications. I didn't know any other way and was desperate to get help, once I was officially diagnosed and realized the extent of my issues. You may find meds necessary in the beginning of your treatment, and then find that the negative side effects of both types of meds are just too much for you. Again, discuss this with your Psychiatrist or Psychopharmacologist. But, be patient and gentle with yourself and please take the time you need to know how these meds affect you.

5 HABITS THAT CAN MAKE YOUR DEPRESSION WORSE

- Inactivity

- Poor Sleep Habits

- Social Isolation

- Poor Diet

- Rumination (negative self-talk/committee in your head)

3 THINGS THAT CONQUER ANXIETY AND DEPRESSION

- Anxiety and Depression: Pandora's Box

- 1 Motivation

- 2. Acceptance

- 3. Mindfulness with goals

ACCEPTANCE

- Own your situation – it's real and needs the light to recognize & heal

- Get professional medical/psychological advice to start your healing journey

- Stop trying to control it or do life on your own when you're struggling

- There's nothing to be ashamed or guilty about: You Matter!

- Plan very achievable short-term goals

- Simplify your routines

- Eliminate overwhelm: take your life down to a simple, manageable core

- Learn basic time-management skills

- Practice mindfulness: become more present and challenge fight-or-flight reactions

- Accept powerlessness – let go of things you can't control

- Stop judging yourself and your condition. Give yourself a break and be gentle with yourself

ACCEPT YOUR LIMITATIONS
It's ok not to be ok
Increase motivation
Accept you're not well
Increase confidence
Accept you can't be as productive
Self demonstrate "can do"
Spend less time procrastinating
Decrease stress
Increase productivity
You can do this

- Take baby steps, but establish basic routines: get out of bed, make food, do some light cleaning, get showered, make lifestyle changes

- Give yourself one simple goal for the day (might be as basic as getting out of bed, washing your face/brushing teeth, taking a walk around the block

- Enjoy activities and exercise to the best of your ability – especially basic exercise: walking around the block everyday, get out of the house, walk in nature

- As hard as it is for many, just taking action: "Move a muscle, change a thought" can make a huge difference in your healing – one step at a time.

- Build a "Can Do" attitude and expand these goals as you build up confidence/ momentum

- Food for Mental Health: Studies show that carefully chosen fruits, vegetables, and dietary supplements can help improve your mental health: Antioxidants Prevent Cell Damage

- "Smart" Carbs Can Have a Calming Effect

- Protein-Rich Foods Boost Alertness

- Try a Mediterranean Diet for B Vitamins

- Get Enough Vitamin D

- Select Selenium-Rich Foods

- Include Omega-3 Fatty Acids

- Your Weight and Lifestyle Matter, Too

- https://www.verywellmind.com/foods-for-depression-4156403

- https://www.webmd.com/depression/guide/diet-recovery#1

- https://www.nutreance.com/articles/redicalm?utm_medium=google_display&utm_campaign=redicalm_ca_content&utm_source=www.webmd.com&utm_term=stress%20symptoms&gclid=EAIaIQobChMIoZa-i--G4gIVkBcBCh1_zAwdEAEYASAAEgKj2_D_BwE

- Believe That Life is Worth Living, and It Will Create the Fact

- by Kavya Hemmanur

- May 1, 2019

- Becoming a scientist, having a doctoral degree had been my dream since I was a kid. I fought really hard, convinced my family that I would take up biotechnology as my majors in my Undergrad. They were little skeptical about my decision but on seeing how determined I was, they agreed. Back then, either becoming a doctor or Computer science engineer were the only career options we had in India. Studying biology in engineering was out of scope. But I did it.

- Taylor's Story of Triumph

- by Taylor Brune

- February 25, 2019

- In 2014, my life was completely turned upside down. Everything I had known before was never to be again. I had been diagnosed with Lyme disease and began treatment immediately. During treatment, my entire life was changed. I had to move out unexpectedly, my relationships with those around me were deteriorating rapidly, and death surrounded me as I grieved loved ones. I felt as if my life was over and I had nothing to fight for.

- Raw Foods to Improve Mood

- Radical Diet Change: The Mediterranean Diet, Keto Diet, the DASH diet Gut-Healing Diet

- What About Supplements?

- Does St. John's Wort Really Work?

- Anti-Inflammatory Supplements to Reduce Depression?

- Self-Help & Life Tools

- Aggressive Self-Care Program, Workout & Exercise, Routines & Rituals, Building Great Support Network incl. friends, family, loved ones)

- Meditation & Mindfulness

- Cognitive and Dialectical Behavioral Therapy

- Attitude Change & Some Helpful Anxiety & Depression Life Hacks

- Developing a Spiritual Journey

- Mediterranean Diet: emphasizes: Eating primarily plant-based foods, such as fruits and vegetables, whole grains, legumes and nuts. Replacing butter with healthy fats such as olive oil and canola oil. Using herbs and spices instead of salt to flavor foods. Limiting red meat to no more than a few times a month.

- Keto Diet The ketogenic diet is a very low-carb, high-fat diet that shares many similarities with the Atkins and low-carb diets. It involves drastically reducing carbohydrate intake and replacing it with fat. This reduction in carbs puts your body into a metabolic state called ketosis.When this happens, your body becomes incredibly efficient at burning fat for energy. It also turns fat into ketones in the liver, which can supply energy for the brain). Ketogenic diets can cause massive reductions in blood sugar and insulin levels. This, along with the increased ketones, has numerous health benefits

- Gut-Healing Diets: There are many, but the premise is that our guts are totally out of alignment and can cause many serious ailments that can make us sick, depressed, anxious, out of balance. Check these solutions out: https://www.google.com/h?rlz=1C1CHBFuyOgge2jKhg&q=best+gut+healing+diets&oq=best+gut+healing+diets&gs_l=psy-ab.3..0i22i30l4.1955.6037..6231...1.0..0.104.1720.21j2......0....1..gws-wiz.... 0i71j35i39j0i67j0j0i131j0i20i263j0i10.gZSy7Aujtso...

- DASHdietTheDASHdietemphasizesportionsize,eatingavarietyoffoodsandgettingtherightamount of nutrients. Discover how DASH can improve your health and lower your blood pressure. https://www.google.com/search?rlz=1C1CHBF_enUS797US801&biw=992&bih=617&ei=ATTQXIO_L4Kk_Qa__LawDw&q=dash+diet&oq=dash+diet&gs_l=psy-ab.3..0i67j0l2j0i20i263j0j0i20i263j0i67j0l3.14514.15919..16056...0.0..0.109.637.8j1......0....1..gws-wiz.......0i71j35i39j0i131j0i10i67.TrxKBHmrvg4

How It Works:

- Substances found naturally in foods change the way your brain releases chemicals that act either as stimulants that help improve your mood or depressants that can contribute to a bad mood. Taste also plays a role; eating foods you enjoy can put you in a good mood, while having to eat foods you don't like can certainly spoil your mood.

- Food scientists have found that bioactive substances, like specific proteins, carbs and vitamins, and certain properties in some foods, including temperature, aroma, and texture, can help relieve stress and enhance your mood. Of course, overeating some of these foods can have the opposite effect.

- Start with Plant Foods, Sip Turmeric Tea, Be Mindful of (Dark) Chocolate, Fill in with Fermented Foods, Enjoy a Little Ice Cream (But Also Yogurt and Buttermilk), Snack on Nuts and Seeds, Smell the Coffee

NUTRITIONAL, HERBAL SUPPLEMENTS

- Top Five Anti Depression Supplements: 1. FISH OIL2. B-COMPLEX VITAMINS, 3. 5-HTP4. THEANINE5. VITAMIN D

- 8 herbs and supplements for depression

- St. John's wort Ginseng, Chamomile, Lavender, Saffron, SAMe, Omega-3 fatty acids, 5-HTP, Folic acid

- Are they effective?

- https://www.mayoclinic.org/diseases-conditions/depression/expert-answers/natural-remedies-for-depression/faq-20058026

- https://www.health.harvard.edu/newsletter_article/Herbal_and_dietary_supplements_for_depression

RADICAL EXERCISE PROGRAM

- Running

- Yoga

- Hiking in the woods

- Zumba

- Pilates

- Kickboxing

- Belly dancing

- Tai chi

- Dancing (any kind)

- Here are 12 ways to get started with your self-care:

- 1. Make sleep part of your self-care routine. 2. Take care of yourself by taking care of your gut. 3. Exercise daily as part of your self-care routine. 4. Eat right for self-care. 5. Say no to others, and say yes to your self-care. 6. Take a self-care trip. 7. Take a self-care break by getting outside. 8. Let a pet help you with your self-care. 9. Take care of yourself by getting organized. 10. Cook at home to care for yourself. 11. Read a book on self-care for self-care. 12. Schedule your self-care time, and guard that time with everything you have.

- https://www.nytimes.com/guides/well/how-to-meditate

- https://www.nytimes.com/guides/well/activity/basic-mindfulness-meditation

- https://www.nytimes.com/guides/well/be-more-mindful-at-work

- https://www.youtube.com/watch?v=6p_yaNFSYaohttps://blog.feedspot.com/meditation_youtube_channels/

- Loneliness & Social Isolation are greatest causes of early death and poor health

- Babies die without touch and social contact – we're social beings

- Building good social connections will help bridge you back to life

- You need tribes of like-minded people struggling with the same problems/issues

- Learn how to have and keep friends

- Learn how to like and love yourself which is first step in liking/loving others

- Force yourself to meet people who can help you and love you till you can love yourself!

- https://www.youtube.com/watch?v=7c5t6FkvUG0
- https://www.ted.com/talks/anjali_kumar_my_failed_mission_to_find_god_and_what_i_found_instead?language=en
- https://www.youtube.com/watch?v=zPB2EC0Z9z4
- https://chopra.com/articles/preparing-your-inner-journey
- https://www.yogiapproved.com/om/hot-to-start-spiritual-practice/
- https://www.youtube.com/watch?v=JEqIFkw-VCk

- https://www.youtube.com/watch?v=7c5t6FkvUG0

- https://www.ted.com/talks/anjali_kumar_my_failed_mission_to_find_god_and_what_i_found_instead?language=en

- https://www.youtube.com/watch?v=zPB2EC0Z9z4

- https://chopra.com/articles/preparing-your-inner-journey

- https://www.yogiapproved.com/om/hot-to-start-spiritual-practice/

- https://www.youtube.com/watch?v=JEqIFkw-VCk

- Move a muscle, change a thought

- How important is it

- Practice acceptance

- Build your self-esteem, self-image, sense of self-worth

- Change Negative to positive self talk

- Identify & Eliminate your roadblocks to change

- Surround yourself with positive people

- Step out of drama and toxicity

- Heal your inner child, set healthy boundaries from toxic parents, siblings, people

- Here's the magic formula:

- Three acts of gratitude. Spend two minutes a day writing down three new things you are grateful for. Do this for 21 days in a row. (Note: The reason this is so powerful is you're training your mind to scan for positives, instead of threats. It's the fastest way of teaching optimism.)

- Journal one positive experience. For two minutes a day, write in detail about one positive experience you've had during the last 24 hours. (This allows your brain to relive it, and teaches your brain that the behavior matters.)

- Exercise. If you hate exercise, here's the good news: All it takes is just 15 minutes of fun cardio activity. (Achor says this is the equivalent of taking an anti-depressant for the first six months, but with a 30 percent lower relapse rate over the next two years. And the reason why exercise is valuable is it trains your brain to believe, "My behavior matters," which is optimism.)

- Breathe. Stop what you're doing, hands off the laptop. Now breathe and watch your breath go in and out for two minutes. Do this every day. This allows your brain to focus on one thing at a time. (Achor says it will "raise accuracy rates, improve levels of happiness, and drop stress levels.")

- Express kindness through a text or email. The most important of the five: For two minutes per day, write a positive email or text praising or thanking someone you know. And do it for a different person each day. (Achor says people who do this become known as positive leaders with strong social connections--the greatest predictor of long-term happiness.)

- By doing these activities to train your brain, the brain releases dopamine and creates a positive mindset for the long term. It will literally reverse the formula for happiness and success.

- http://www.shawnachor.com/in-action/oprah-happiness-ecourse/ https://www.youtube.com/watch?v=wr4QlxoN2tY http://www.oprah.com/own-super-soul-sunday/shawn-achor-2-ways-to-be-happier-today-video

- 21-Day Happiness Workout & Kickstart and the amazing 7-Step Happiness Mastery Course are available from The Healing Academy

- Follow our 10 simple tips to help manage and reduce your stress levels.

- Avoid Caffeine, Alcohol, and Nicotine. …

- Indulge in Physical Activity. …

- Get More Sleep. …

- Try Relaxation Techniques. …

- Talk to Someone. …

- Keep a Stress Diary. …

- Take Control. …

- Manage Your Time.

- Learn to say "NO"

- Rest when your ill

- What is the purpose of your life? Purpose can guide life decisions, influence behavior, shape goals, offer a sense of direction, and create meaning. For some people, purpose is connected to vocation—meaningful, satisfying work. For others, their purpose lies in their responsibilities to their family or friends.

- What makes a meaningful life? When people explain what makes their lives meaningful, they tend to describe four things: having rich relationships and bonds to others; having something worthwhile to do with their time; crafting narratives that help them understand themselves and the world they live in; and having experiences of awe and wonder.

- https://www.ted.com/playlists/313/talks_to_help_you_find_your_pu

- https://www.ted.com/talks/rick_warren_on_a_life_of_purpose?language=en

- https://www.ted.com/talks/emily_esfahani_smith_there_s_more_to_life_than_being_happy?language=en

- https://www.ted.com/talks/philip_krinks_finding_your_personal_mission_in_life

- Cinema Therapy: According to Psycom experts:

- Love Actually, The Sound of Music, Singing in the Rain, Guys & Dolls, Silver Linings Playbook, Bringing Up Baby, Terms of Endearment, E.T. (Extra-Terrestrial), Whey Harry Met Sally, The Producers, Annie, Practical Magic, Mrs. Doubtfire. There are many more inspirational, uplifting, hope-filled movies to pick from,

- Music Therapy. Click on these:

- https://www.youtube.com/watch?v=YRoAlMZTeyE

- https://www.youtube.com/watch?v=J3Jb2t7aD2U

- https://www.youtube.com/watch?v=nFwkeOyYV1I

- https://themighty.com/2017/08/anxiety-depression-songs/

Routine
CAFETERIA
Cue
Reward

HOW DO YOU FEEL RIGHT NOW?

- Do you feel raw? Like you've been worked over?

- Are you uncertain what to do with these uncomfortable feelings?

- The results of your buried, often unresolved past can be shocking and difficult

- Talk with a trusted advisor/friend, professional

- Keep doing the work of change!

SUMMARY AND CONGRATULATIONS

HOW TO KNOW IF YOU'RE HEALING

GIVE YOURSELF A BIG HUG/PAT ON THE BACK

KEEP PRACTICING MORE OF A GOOD THING

YOU ARE GOOD. NOW IT'S TIME TO KNOW IT FOR REAL!

NEXT STEPS ON YOUR HEALING JOURNEY

- THE HEALING ACADEMY (url)/facebook group)

- Healing from Toxic Parents

- Happiness Mastery System

- 21-Day Happiness Challenge

- Making Love Work

- Making Life Work

- Spiritual Journey

- Mindfulness & Meditation

- All my e-books

THANKS